I0456100

SOCIETY IN A MARKET ECONOMY

George Kopelas

authorHOUSE®

AuthorHouse™ UK Ltd.
500 Avebury Boulevard
Central Milton Keynes, MK9 2BE
www.authorhouse.co.uk
Phone: 08001974150

© 2011 George Kopelas. All rights reserved.

No part of this book may be reproduced, stored in a retrieval system, or transmitted by any means without the written permission of the author.

First published by AuthorHouse 02/14/2011.

ISBN: 978-1-4520-7184-8 (sc)

This book is printed on acid-free paper.

Contents

Society and Individuals

The true value of people and things is revealed during their absence

Society is an aggregate of individuals bound together by location, history, trade, common ownership, joy or sorrow. From the point of view of a scientist, any individual in relation to society is nothing more than a word in a book, a digit in a number, a line in a drawing, a tree in a forest, or a star in the sky. Certain individuals may be very different from the others, or more important to society but no individual can determine the existence or the course of a society **as an individual**. On the contrary, society can determine not only the life styles and roles of individuals but also the very existence of any member. No individual is precluded from the hazards of local crime, political terror, bad medical care and public transport (the lives of airplane passengers are determined by pilots, airtraffic controllers and maintenance workers).

The study of human history has revealed the existence of thousands of men who have made a significant contribution to the development of civilization. From a mathematical point of view each individual is a real number, positive or negative, small or large but always a definite number while society is the infinity.

Similarly, from a physical point of view man is a star while society is a galaxy. Man is a cloud in the sky, a cell in the body of a society, a small part of grand total.

So far, all individuals have had a definitive life span not exceeding that of a few generations while societies such as nations have existed for thousands of years. Millions died during the Second World War in an effort to keep the existing societies intact while no society has ever endangered itself for the survival of any single member, even for its absolute ruler. "The King is dead, long live the King!" All societies praise the heros returning from the battle-field but no society praises, or even tolerates a despot or tyrant for long. (The car as a whole is more important than any of its components).

Personal Relations and Interdependence

We all owe something to the society

From the moment we were born we all became a burden to society and particularly to our parents (in fact, we all became a burden to our mother from the first days of conception). During the first years of our life we were all fed and taken care of by others for the return of a few smiles on our part. Was that enough for our parents? Probably yes. Is that enough for our society? Certainly not!

If we were all living on the provisions of older generations we should soon have to turn the clock of history back to the era when man was hunting in forests and slept in caves. Since none of us is eager to dispense with the comforts of modern technology and mass production, we are all prepared. To participate in the creation of new wealth for our own sake.

Individuals hardly contribute equally to a common end even if they all want to do so (we are all constrained by our physical and mental capacity as well as by our own level of experience). The practical question as to "how the end product will be divided or shared by all" remains the cause of friction and conflict until resolved in a manner acceptable to the strongest (the lion's share).

In real life, the law is nothing more than the right of the strong. Actually, the law is full of duties, responsibilities and obligations on the part of the many who struggle for survival. Nevertheless, no individual can survive and enjoy life away from society. Even monks and nuns live in groups, for individual needs are best satisfied through common effort. Man is a social animal. For that reason, dangerous criminals and political adversaries who are not executed but condemned to a sentence for life imprisonment are all placed under solitary confinement.

Public Life, Freedom and Legislation

Freedom is a matter of relative strength

Public life consists of every individual activity which is readily recognized as significantly affecting the interests of all members of society. All individuals are affected by public life even if they find it boring or uninteresting.

Freedom is usually considered the absence of any social constraints on individual behaviour. In reality, however, freedom is nothing more than our ability to determine our personal life.

Freedom is not absolute. It depends upon various factors such as our physical and mental condition, our level of education and experience, the environment in which we live and the means we have at our disposal. A baby is not so free as his mother, a student is not so free as his teacher, a soldier is not so free as his captain, a worker is not so free as his manager etc (the more we depend on others the less free we are). In fact, we are all less free than we usually think. How many times have we all tried to get out of habits such as smoking and drinking and failed?

Political freedom is our capacity to do certain things as members of an organized society irrespective of our personal abilities and private means. "In the eyes of law all individuals are equal". In reality, however, the law as a rule refers to what we are allowed or not allowed to do irrespective of our physical, mental, and financial capacity. Political freedom appears as the ability to choose between various alternatives, a right of choice rather than a right of action.

The law merely provides the "rules of the game". The law does not guarantee that there will be a fair play (that depends upon the relative strength and moral standards of the players).

The law provides the field in which we may move as we please but not the means for doing so. One may move around the country on foot, on a bicycle, on a car, train or jet. The richer you are the more swiftly you can move.

The same discrimination applies to most provisions of life such as food, accommodation, education and entertainment. In a society where the ownership of the means of production is in private hands the civil liberties are actually determined by the distribution of property rights and money among the population. Thus, a real increase in one's private wealth automatically brings about an increase in one's personal freedom.

Human Life and Human Needs

No need, no life

A living organism (plant or animal) is something that is frequently changing in shape, size and substance. In good time, it moves, transforms, grows and shrinks.

Man, the most complex of all animals on Earth, is not excepted from the Laws of Nature governing life. Therefore, a comprehensive study of human life must take into account the findings of Natural Sciences such as Physics, Chemistry and Biology. For that reason, our study of human society must begin with the examination of human life from the point of view of a natural scientist.

No man can survive long without replenishing in his body the watter he has consumed (i.e. he has to eat food and drink watter on a regular basis). In addition, he has to keep his body temperature steady at 36.6oC. These provisions for the preservation of human life are known as "basic human needs" and call for the consumption of certain kinds of good, the wearing of clothes, the construction of houses etc. Furthermore, man in order to survive as a species must reproduce himself through sex and child-birth and live as a member of a group of individuals, (i.e. in a society).

Life is a continuous process of exchange between man and Nature as well as between people. In that context, human needs may be divided in two categories depending on their sources of origin.

I) Those stemming from the effects of exchange between man and Nature such as hunger and thirst. They are commonly known as physiological needs. They are the concern of biologists and physicians.

II) Those stemming from the effects of exchange and interaction between individuals such as love and respect. They are commonly known as psychological needs. They are the concern of sociologists and psychologists.

Politicians are concerned with both, and so should you!

The Laws of Nature, and Human Needs and Drives

Man is a tiny part of the Universe

Man, being nothing more than a small part of Nature, is governed by the laws that apply to all matter in the Universe.

Since man is the most complex of all entities on Earth, he is simultaneously affected by a group of natural forces such as Gravity and Electromagnetism. Individuals with a relatively weak intellectual capacity provide good examples of the influence of such forces on mankind. Gravity may produce personal inadequacies such as gluttony, covetousness, stinginess, lust and egoism. Sloth, apathy and conservatism are phenomena of Inertia on the homo sapiens. On the other hand, Electromagnetism produces social phenomena such as fiestas, sports and riots, and on a smaller scale sexual attraction, love, sympathy and charity as well as their opposites such as intolerance and hate. All "deep" human feelings are chemical reactions produced by physical forces.

The emotions are a form of energy. But energy is nothing more than matter in motion. Thus, love is a chemical reaction produced by physical attraction due to Electromagnetism. In fact, the difference between energy and matter is a matter of speed. Subsequently, nuclear energy is defined as the movement of the smallest particles of matter at exceptionally high speeds. On the other hand, the human spirit is nothing more than energy stemming from the brain, whereas the human soul represents an aggregate of the nerves and blood systems in each individual as they function. Thoughts and ideas are products of brain energy.

Psychology in order to explain human behaviour named certain "internal" forces as drives and motives. They differ from individual to individual in terms of direction, intensity and timing.

Human Needs and Values

Man is driven either by love or by self-interest

Although the so-called basic human needs are common to all men, there are numerous ways to satisfy them.

If you want to satisfy your hunger in a restaurant, you may choose from a dozen of dishes and then eat various quantities from the same menu. Thus, there are thousands of ways to satisfy a simple need such as nutrition. The same applies to entertainment: you may watch T.V., go to the theatre, go to the movies, go driving, go swimming, go climbing, go skiing, go riding, go dancing, go shopping, play tennis, chess etc. and in each case choose a different place or companion for the same purpose. But how do we choose among so many alternatives?

In each case we have to give up some of our limited time of life in return for a new experience. In each case there is a personal benefit at a certain cost. From the point of view of the consumer, the benefit is an "input" an "income", whereas the cost is an "output", an "expense".

Thinking in accounting terms, the difference amounts to a net profit or loss depending on whether we feel better or worse than before. Everyday we have to make thousands of choices among the words to use in speech, what or whom to see, where to go and what to do. Every alternative is a proposition to accept or reject. Every minute we are awake we consider, either consciously or subconsciously, a great number of various propositions. Each proposition is expected to yield a definite outcome in terms of personal satisfaction (utility) or dissatisfaction. This expected outcome in subjective terms gives rise to the development of a valuation system which serves as a blueprint for action.

Every possible course of action is considered and evaluated, even subconsciously, before a choice is made. Since such evaluation aims at personal satisfaction, each individual develops his own standards for comparison in accordance with his individual needs and background ("beauty is in the eye of the beholder!"). The way people do their shopping is characteristic of the differences among individuals.

Property Rights

Ownership is not a natural right but a social concession

The preservation of human life is impossible without recourse to Nature. We cannot survive without oxygen for more than 5 minutes, without water for more than 2 weeks and without food for more than 2 months. Since man is so dependent upon his environment for his survival, he makes every effort to control and use it to his own advantage.

Man cannot survive for long as an individual. He has to live in groups with other people in order to face the hazards of life more successfully. The need for a common effort in order to preserve and enjoy life gives rise to the formation of communities. The establishment of communities and the need to appropriate the products of common effort call for the formation of a definite set of rules that regulate social contacts and determine individual relationships with the various utilities (useful things).

When all things are available to everybody at all times we have a communist society. In that case no individual enjoys a special relationship with any of the existing useful things (dwellings, clothes, food, water etc). Everything is controlled by everybody and everybody enjoys everything. (This is an ideal situation, a model). In practice, however, in a big community consisting of thousands, public control of small or perishable things is not effective in the long run. For practical reasons, it is necessary to establish a set of rules that regulate the relationships between the various individuals on one hand and the available wealth on the other (i.e. all the useful things collectively). The above rules are known as property laws and the control relationships thereof as property rights. A permanent and absolute control over things is known as ownership, whereas a temporary and conditional control over things is known as possession. Control over the various things may pass from one person to another under a set of rules known as Contract Law. When certain things are permanently controlled by a definite group of individuals (or individual) they are known as private property. Subsequently, all the other things considered together constitute what is known as public property (common property).

Since property laws deal with the most vital interests of the community, it was a matter of relative strength and persuasion to determine the rules that regulated the assignment of property rights to the various individuals. It was like determining the lion's share. In the end, the strongest took the most and the weakest almost nothing.

The first things to be owned privately were small portable things such as weapons and clothes. Originally, they were in the possession of the finders ("finders-keepers"). They were usually found in a primitive form and had to be improved through elaborate manual work in order to acquire a more convenient shape and size. Thus, labour increased the usefulness of things (i.e. it added to their value in use).

The weapons were used to add to one's physical strength. Since physical strength was indispensable in maintaining control over possessions, weapons soon became the means to obtain possession of things through force. Naturally, the greatest warriors in tribes became the first chieftains, and then kings. This led from a communist society to an oligarchy, and then to a monarchy. Moreover, the development of technology led to an increase in private property not only in the form of land ownership but also in the form of commodities. The huge accumulation of commodities in private hands is a characteristic of the capitalist society.

Useful Goods and Utility

Too much of a good is bad

Most human needs are satisfied through various objects such as clothes, vehicles, electronics etc. For that purpose, they are all regarded as useful goods.

Useful goods do not give the same amount of satisfaction to different people. In fact, then do not give the same amount of satisfaction even to the same person at different points in time. We all know that a glass of water is a source of satisfaction to a thirsty man. Nevertheless, if that man keeps drinking a glass of water every ten minutes at the end of the hour the water will turn into a source of torture. Thus, the same good may be a source of satisfaction or dissatisfaction according to the circumstances. In economics, that satisfaction is called utility.

The utility of a good is something subjective and varies by time. After a certain point, the more we consume of the same good the less satisfaction we derive from its use. This applies to all useful goods (law of diminishing marginal utility).

The Distribution of Wealth, and the Utility of Goods and Leisure

Appreciation is a matter of deprivation

Utility is not only a matter of personal taste but also of position. The richer you are the lower the utility of a particular product (diminishes by consuming similar goods during the same period).

Consumption takes time. The richer you are the more time you need to enjoy your possessions ("time is money"). Unfortunately, time is available in limited quantities. Time has no substitutes and is a necessary good. Moreover, it is a complementary good (consumed together with other goods). Consequently, as private wealth increases so does the utility of leisure.

On the contrary, time stands very low in the eyes of the unemployed. They have plenty of time but only a few material possessions. They are rich in time but poor in all other respects.

Utilities and Values

Knowledge is a child of experience and reason

From the point of view of the consumer, utility becomes more meaningful and useful when it is expressed in quantitative terms. But this is only possible when different utilities of the same consumer are compared at the same time. In that case, the consumer compares definite quantities of different goods using something useful as a standard unit of account. All goods but one are expressed as equivalent to that good in various proportions. The quantitative relationships so derived are known as values. In short, they express the capacity of objects to satisfy human needs. So long as human needs vary from individual to individual, for the same bundle of goods each individual will produce a different set of values.

The above values are entirely subjective, for they are products of personal calculations aimed at developing an evaluation system that would maximize personal satisfaction. They have no relation to market values, which are products of social negotiations.

Values and Money

Value is a matter of social contribution

Since most goods are valued differently by each individual, society as a whole will be better off if each good is consumed by the individual who appreciates it most. But individual values can only be expressed quantitatively and objectively if they are compared to a standard value. When that standard value is adopted and used by all members of society, it takes the form of something known as money.

As soon as a particular good is accepted as money, it is possible for all individuals to produce a utility function for each available good in terms of a common value. In the end, all goods will be valued in terms of money, though differently by each individual.

Goods and Trade

To sell means to offer for one's own benefit

It usually happens that two individuals are in possession and control of different goods and in different quantities. Considering their position they may feel that they would be both better off if their goods were more evenly distributed. In that case they will consider to exchange part of the goods possessed in relative abundance. For instance, a farmer in possession of a store of wheat may feel better off if he exchanges part of his stock for the cheese produced by a shepherd. The latter may also feel better off if he exchanges part of his stock of cheese for a number of sacks of wheat. But how much cheese to exchange for one sack of wheat?

The shepherd will obviously benefit by giving up as little cheese as possible for each sack of wheat while the opposite holds true for the farmer. In a bargain "one man's gain is another man's loss". The rate of exchange will only by fixed if they are both satisfied from the bargain. But for a bargain to be reached they need not be **equally** satisfied! It suffices that they both feel that they will be better off than before.

The systematic exchange of property rights over goods possessed in relative abundance (or less wanted) is known as trade. In a society characterized by private property the exchange of goods between individuals is a norm of the everyday life. Each individual tries to maximize the utility of his possessions through exchange. Goods change hands until they reach the individual who wants them most (and for that reason values them most).

Values and Trade

The discovery of the truth calls for a departure from the fascinating world of fiction

When the farmer exchanges his wheat for cheese he feels that he increases the total utility of his personal wealth. The same is felt by the shepherd, who gives up some of his cheese for more bread. The values received are known as income whereas the values given up are known as costs. The difference between income and cost is known as profit (or loss, if negative).

In the above case both traders feel that they make a profit (increase the total value of their wealth). But this is a subjective approach. For an outsider it is irrelevant whether a particular loaf of breed or piece of cheese belongs to the farmer or the shepherd. For an outsider there is no change in values! As long as values remain quantitative expressions of utilities they can have an effect only on the traders involved. However, in a society where trade is effected through the use of money, all values are expressed in money terms and, therefore, all goods obtained through exchange have an objective value. That value is known as price. That price is an income to the seller and a cost, or expense, to the buyer. Obviously, a trader cannot make a profit unless he sells his goods for prices much higher than those paid for their acquisition.

The Market

Every dollar spent on the purchase of a good is also a vote for its production

The market is an aggregate of actual products and potential traders. Acting as a bridge between producers and consumers it facilitates the distribution of private surplus wealth. Its very existence depends on the use of a single good as a medium of exchange and store of values (i.e. money).

In primitive societies the market was a particular area for trading all sorts of goods. Improvements in transport and communications during the Industrial Revolution led to the formation of markets for specific commodities (wheat, cotton, wool, silver, gold etc) known by the name of the product to be traded and not by the place of exchange. Markets such as the market for gold and oil attract nowadays traders from all over the world. Although they are based on specific cities, they are, in fact, world markets.

The economies in which money is used in all productive and commercial activities are known as market economies.

Demand and Supply

Trade primarily serves the needs of the rich

The supply of money in exchange for goods and services is known as demand, whereas the supply of goods and services in exchange for money is simply known as supply. Market prices are determined by demand and supply.

Demand is not the mere want for goods or services but their acquisition or use in exchange for money. In terms of certainty, in a bargain the cash holder enjoys an advantage over the seller. The potential buyer knows the exact value of his negotiating good (i.e. money) because he knows the value (price) of dozens of goods he can obtain in exchange. The seller, however, is in possession of a good with an uncertain value (it will be determined by the actual buyer himself). This is known as consumers' sovereignty.

The Distribution of Wealth
and Bargaining Positions

Profits beget wealth, and wealth begets profits

In a market economy people try to maximize the utility of their personal wealth by increasing or decreasing their cash holdings in exchange for goods (selling goods when their utility falls below their selling price and buying goods when their expected utility rises above their cost). However, as their personal wealth increases in quantity and variety they find that the utility of any particular good in their possession diminishes. On the other hand, those who become poorer and poorer find that the utility of their possessions increases by time!

The same applies to money. As people become richer and richer the utility of a certain amount of money decreases and increases again when they go bankrupt. In the ordinary course of business, the utility of money is greater for the poor and smaller for the rich. As a result, the barons of industry and commerce can afford to buy their stocks at a discount and sell them below market prices or hoard them until they rise to a certain level. In contrast, the small producers and shopkeepers are compelled to accept market prices and even sell at a discount when they are short of cash.

The utility of leisure, however, is directly proportional to one's own wealth. It is high for the rich and low for the poor. The rich have everything to spare but time while the poor have nothing to spare but their miserable lives. Time is the only good the rich find worth buying from the poor. "Time is money" claim the millionaires, and they are quite right. The price to be paid for such a time is known in the labour market as wages.

The utility of wages depends upon the financial position of workers and their propensity to consume. Since poverty and advertising tend to increase the utility of cash holdings, the poorer the workers the higher the utility of their wages. Therefore, the rich have every reason to keep the level of wages as low as possible.

The above demonstrate that bargaining positions are primarily determined by three factors:

First, the personal needs and preferences of the negotiating parties. Personal needs and preferences determine the evaluation system used by each negotiator. Every consumer trader develops his own utility schedule and thereby his own evaluation system. Then, he chooses among various alternatives in order to maximize his total utility (satisfaction). Advertising aims at changing the utility schedules of consumers through changes in personal needs, drives and preferences.

Second, their current levels of consumption (Law of Inertia). Consumers tend to develop a fairly steady consumption pattern in accordance with their personal needs and drives.

Third, their personal wealth (including stock levels held at the time of negotiation). In fact, the aim of exchange is the increase in the value of the traders' personal wealth as evaluated **by themselves**. The greater their wealth the stronger their bargaining positions. Moreover, the stronger their bargaining positions the greater the profits to be made from the particular transactions (as the weaker parties are more anxious to conclude the deals).

Production and Work

Work is the mother of prosperity

Production is the process whereby various materials are combined together in a definite way to form a new object with new qualities. The objects so formed are known as products. They may be divided into natural products (formed without the intervention of man), agricultural products (man intervenes in the natural process), industrial products (man using advanced technology develops and controls the process) and cultural products (when man primarily uses his intellect to produce things and ideas that satisfy the human soul and spirit. This book is such a product).

Industrial production is dependent upon various human activities and efforts, known as work and labour. The same applies to agricultural production, which is also influenced by natural forces. No production is possible without some kind of work (even the collection of natural production is itself a kind of work).

Work may be divided into manual work (usually called labour) and intellectual work. Nevertheless, any kind of work involves the simultaneous use of the body and mind, the difference lying in the degree to which the body and mind are used and the expertise required. A farmer does not have to use much of his mind at work whereas a civil engineer does not have to use much of his body. An operating surgeon, however, has to use both his body and mind very carefully and skilfully.

People work in order to produce the things required to satisfy their wants. Cultural production can sometimes be a single man's job but industrial and agricultural productions call for the cooperation of a number of workers to perform different tasks at the same time. Besides, specialization at work tends to improve craftsmanship and increase efficiency. It is also necessary for the use of advanced technology. In industry, the breaking up of a productive process into a large number of separate jobs with each worker specializing in a single operation is known as division of labour.

Cooperation versus Competition

Competition is the salt of life

In the business world, cooperation means to work together and share the fruits of labour in a manner arranged beforehand. Competition, on the other hand, means to work for oneself and try to gain from the others as much as possible.

Since most production calls for a coordinated effort on the part of a number of workers, most of them usually have to work in groups under common management and direction. Then they may form a group of workers with equal rights and duties, a business known as general partnership.

A general partnership raises important managerial and financial issues, the following:

First, all members must agree as to what work is to be done and how (planning).

Second, they must all agree about the specific job each of them is going to do (organisation).

Third, they must all be satisfied with everybody's job (control).

Fourth, they must all contribute to the expenses as agreed.

Fifth, they must all share in the profits as agreed.

Obviously, the greater the number of partners the greater the number of problems in a partnership. Nevertheless, a large partnership offers financial security to its members in case of personal misfortunes. Its prosperity will not be jeopardized by the temporary absence of a single member, and any subsequent reduction in profits will be sustained by all members without prejudice.

Partnerships usually suffer from lack of effective control. If a partner is misbehaving he cannot be forced to comply or resign until all the other partners turn against him. But this is very unlikely until hard evidence has been collected, something very difficult in a business where everybody has easy access to all documents and records. Moreover, the distribution of profits and losses among a considerable number of people does not provide an incentive for harder work. Some may feel that their contribution to the business in terms of individual work is above the average, and ask for more, or offer less. This will soon end up in falling production levels, or quality standards.

Competitive conditions develop when a number of traders of the same kind of product (or service) negotiate simultaneously with another party. Under such conditions the traders may have to lower the price of their products in order to gain customers. Competitive selling is beneficial for buyers, whereas competitive bidding is good for sellers. Obviously, a competitive market presumes the existence of a large number of small traders on both sides who operate independently from each other. In reality, however, traders tend to combine on both sides, especially when the gains from doing so are significant. A combination of sellers may restrict supply volumes so that prices settle at premium levels (e.g. OPEC agreements in the 1970's). On the other hand, consumers may agree to reduce their purchases of a certain good until its price collapses (e.g. oil prices in the 1980's).

Business experience has shown that the position of the financially strongest prevails in trade agreements. The poor and weak have to succumb to the terms of the rich and strong.

Trade competition stems from private property, and leads to financial and social inequality. It provides incentives for harder work on the part of the poor, but not for the rich.

Land and Capital

Nothing stems from nowhere

Capital is the accumulation of values in a certain material form. Thus, financial capital is the accumulation of values in the form of money, commercial capital is in the form of commodities, industrial capital in the form of technological equipment etc. Apart from modern financial capital, all capital is a joint product of manual labour and scientific work. However, only industrial capital directly contributes to the production of more wealth (useful things considered collectively).

The use of land is necessary for the production of food and for the extraction of minerals to be used in industry.

All industrial products consist of materials found on the Earth and processed by workers with the use of the appropriate equipment. For that reason, land, labour and capital are collectively known as the factors of production.

Private land ownership transformed the primitive communist societies into societies ruled by landlords (known as aristocrats under the feudal system). Similarly, private capital ownership with the help of advanced technology transformed the feudal societies into societies ruled by merchants, industrialists and financiers (collectively known as capitalists). In both cases labour was used as a supplier of working hands and heads while production was planned, organised, directed and controlled by the land or capital owners. The latter enjoyed the lion's share in the wealth produced.

In the societies that abolished private ownership of land and capital (under communism) the role of landlords and capitalists was played by the ruling political leaderships in those societies (the governments formed by the Communist Parties).

Communism versus Private Enterprise

Equality and ideals are children of imagination

Under communism there is no private ownership of the means of production (land and capital). Every member of a communist society has the right to share the fruits of labour as if he were a general partner in a large partnership. The same applies to his duties. Obviously, the issues that arise in a large partnership also arise in a communist state. Thus, there must be a general consensus regarding the planning, organisation, direction and control of all production in the society. This amounts to an unanimous reply to the following questions:

"What is to be produced, in what specifications and how much?"

"What job is to be done by each member of society?"

"Who shall bear the costs for failing to meet production targets?"

"How are the goods produced to be distributed?"

Communist states, like large partnerships, suffer from lack of effective control over misbehaving citizens (especially when they are placed in high positions). Besides, no system is more efficient than the market system to determine what the people really want, and in what quantities and specifications. In any case, some form of private ownership is necessary for the distribution of goods which cannot be used by people living at a distance, or as an incentive for keeping durable goods in good condition (industrial equipment, accommodation units, motor vehicles etc). Even in a communist state there will be times when some people will actually have considerable authority over others (parents over children, teachers over students, naval officers over seamen, civil engineers over construction workers, doctors over nurses etc). This is equivalent to a de facto recognition of special rights. Thus, even in a communist state the rights and duties are not equally distributed. Some people will inevitably enjoy a greater share in the National Product, even if that is not formally recognized or accepted because of their position in the process of production and distribution.

A communist state does not claim complete abolition of all privileges but a system of government that provides its citizens with equal opportunities and means for any career. Under communism, children have a right to free education, accommodation, food, and travel. All adults have a right to employment and a duty to work. Everyone has easy access to social and cultural events and enjoys free medical care.

A communist state aspires to eliminate the conditions for great differences in individual incomes and wealth. It is a model state rather than an actual one. It is presumed that it will decay soon after industrial production rises above a certain level.

Under private enterprise there are no legal limits as to the amount of wealth an individual is allowed to own. Moreover, the individual has the right to use and dispose of his property at will. The ownership of private wealth may be transferred freely from individual to individual without social or political interference. Traders can set prices at will, and parents can pass most of their property rights to their children. Thus, people may be born very rich or poor, and lead a life determined by personal fortune rather than merit. In addition, nobody has a legal obligation to work (e.g. the members of a royal family do not have to work in order to enjoy a luxurious life style). In fact, under private enterprise most property rights are not acquired but inherited.

In a market economy money serves as a right to all goods and services. The people who are not born rich have to work very hard in order to earn their right to decent accommodation and advanced education. Employment is not a right guaranteed by the capitalist state. People may find no demand for their labour and remain unemployed for years, or accept positions that do not do them justice. Unemployment and underemployment are common experience in a market economy.

Production and Distribution

In our competitive world most athletes still run barefoot

The production of goods calls for a series of definite movements and actions on the part of producers. They have to spend a considerable amount of time and energy during the process. This, in turn, calls for a reward which more than compensates for those losses. For that reason, the value of their reward must be greater than the sum total of the values consumed in the process (known as the costs of production).

In a market economy all economic activity aims at increasing the producers' estate. The producers may be either owners of the business or outside workers who offer their services under a contract of employment. The owners' reward is known as profit, whereas the employees' reward is known as wages or salaries.

The level of wages and salaries (the price of labour) is a matter of negotiation between the owners of the business or their agents (managers) and the workers or their representatives (union leaders). Subsequently, the workers offer their productive capacity to their employers, who use them for their own benefit (to make a profit) in return for a sum of money that will compensate them for the time lost and the energy expended for the enterprise. The poorer the workers the lower the level of wages they are prepared to accept! (The poorer they are the greater the cost of being unemployed, and therefore the greater the "profits" gained from employment even at a low wage level). Moreover, the lower the wages the higher the profits of the business. Consequently, the poorer the workers the richer the business owners (capitalists).

While the labour owners (i.e. workers) lend themselves to the business owners for a certain number of hours per day, the lend owners land their land to the land users in return for a fixed reward per month known as rent. Similarly, the cash holders may lend their money for a fixed reward per period, which is known as interest.

In summary, wages, salaries, profits, interest and rent are all rewards for participating in the production process. All, but profits, are fixed in advance and certain in amount.

The Forms of Money

Money is a right

All goods are produced in order to satisfy human wants. Food is produced to provide the human body with the proteins and calories required for its preservation. Clothes are made to protect our body from low temperatures. Houses are built to protect us from the rain and snow. Motor cars, trains, ships and airplanes are manufactured to increase the speed of traffic. In summary, all products are made in order to make our life more enjoyable, longer or less unpleasant.

Most products have a life span much shorter than ours. They can be useful for a limited number of days, either because they perish or wear out or because new products offer more for the same price. Thus, producers enjoying a surplus of produce have the following options:

First, keep their surplus in storage for a possible future use.

Second, exchange it without delay for something that has a fairly steady value over time and is in general demand (i.e. money). In this case the producers can assure the value of their surplus produce while the consumers have the chance to enjoy the fruits of production fresh and without delay. Obviously, this is a better option under normal conditions.

Naturally, the first goods to be used as money were certain minerals which were in general use and demand, and whose properties did not diminish by time. Durability, utility, stability, portability, divisibility, purity and scarcity are indispensable properties of good money. Salt, copper, silver and gold possess those properties and were successively used as money for many centuries. Before long, for handling purposes and for the preservation of purity the coinage system was developed whereby the metal to be used as money was moulded in useful shapes and denominations of a prescribed standard weight bearing the appropriate official stamps on their face as a guarantee for their genuineness (i.e. coins).

Coins may serve well as money so long as their face value remains greater than their intrinsic value. When their face value falls below their intrinsic value they are worth more as metals than mediums of exchange, and subsequently cash holders hoard them as stores of appreciating values.

That may happen when some of the coins in circulation are made from precious metals while the other coins are base (bad money drives out good!).

The use of a single metal in coinage does not guarantee a steady value for money. An increase in the demand for the metal will reduce its supply for coinage. Besides, a constant supply of money in an expanding economy will soon lead to a fall in the general level of prices (which is equivalent to a rise in the value of money). On the other hand, a continuous fall in the value of money (i.e. inflation) reduces the value of cash and savings.

During the Industrial Revolution gold coins became the principal form of money. Then, for safety reasons, cash holders started to deposit their savings with local goldsmiths in return for a receipt. The latter was a written promise by the goldsmiths to pay on demand a specified amount of money in cash (i.e. gold coins). In time, goldsmiths found that they could lend part of that cash to other traders, who used it again to finance their purchases from other merchants. It was not long before goldsmiths turned into businessmen engaged in borrowing and lending funds (i.e. acting as bankers) issuing promissory notes (i.e. bank notes) for cash deposits. In retrospect, paper money is a product of the banking system.

Paper money has no intrinsic value. It represents a debt of the issuing bank towards the note bearer. After the Second World War all paper money has been issued by the state banks (known as central banks). In this respect, paper money represents state debts in circulation. Commercial bank deposits, on the other hand, represent commercial bank debt.

Nowadays, commercial bank deposits and bank notes in circulation comprise the principal forms of money in use (personal cheques are transfer orders for bank deposits). Apart from coins, all money represents transferable impersonal debt.

The Value of Money Today

Motion is life, rest is death

The value of a good is the measure of its capacity to satisfy human wants. Consequently, the value of money is equal to the value of goods it can provide in exchange. In a market economy a certain amount of money may be exchanged for various quantities and types of goods depending on the taste and preferences of the spender. With the exception of coins, the value of money is nothing more than its purchasing power. Thus, an increase in bank notes and deposits does not increase the total value of money, for their value is associated with the wealth of the society. If that wealth remains stable over the years, an increase in the supply of money will soon result in an increase in the general level of prices and therefore to a fall in the value of money, as more money will be required for the purchase of the same goods. Nevertheless, in an expanding economy a small increase in the supply of money is necessary in order to absorb the extra production of goods without a fall in the general level of prices (i.e. a rise in the value of money).

Income and Expenditure

Whatever we do affects both our surroundings and ourselves

The inflow of money in exchange for goods and services supplied is known as income, the reverse as expenditure. Thus, wages and salaries represent an income to the workers and an expenditure (or expense) to their employers, rent an income to the land owners and an expense to their tenants, and interest represents an income to money lenders and an expenditure to their debtors. Profit, however, is not an income in itself but the excess of income over expenditure during a certain period of time (accounting profit is the increase in the value of the owner's equity in the course of business).

Expenditure for Consumption and Investment

If you want to enjoy the present you have to prepare for the future, for the present is a future of the past

The use of goods for the direct satisfaction of human needs is known as consumption. On the other hand, certain goods are used as aids for the production of other goods. For instance, the anvil and hammer are used by the blacksmith to help him give shape to heated metals; the spinning wheel and the spindle are used as aids to form threads; the factory to protect workers and machinery from rain and snow. The expenditure of money for the production or acquisition of such goods is known as investment. Such goods are known as capital goods and are exclusively used for the production of wealth. All industrial machinery and tools are capital goods.

Income and Work

To work means to serve society

Money, as any other good, may be used by its holder on the first days of its acquisition (i.e. spent) or stored for a future use (i.e. saved) depending on the personality of the holder, his income, his financial commitments, his wealth, his health, his life style, his expectations etc. The higher his current income the lower the marginal value of any specific increase in his remunaration, for everybody buys first the things he wants most. This has vast consequences in productivity, for income above a certain level ceases to operate effectively as an incentive for more work. (People tend to identify employment with work but this is not necessarily so; a worker may be a full-time employee but offer very little work). Thus, exceptionally high incomes do not necessarily correspond to precious individual work. Unfortunately, there is often a tendency by high income earners to overvalue their individual contribution in business by taking credit for the work performed by their subordinates.

Industrial Capital and Profits

Knowledge and money have a tendency to accumulate

All industrial capital is a joint product of manual labour and scientific work. Its use aims at increasing the volume of production per man employed (i.e. increase productivity). The extensive use of capital equipment in industry and agriculture in the last two centuries raised productivity to unprecedented levels. In the mean time, vast improvements in the means of transport and communications led to a huge growth in trade and markets. The huge development of information technology provided for the globalization of business activities. In the end, the extensive use of capital changed not only the conditions at work but also those of our private lives.

Under private enterprise most of the industrial capital is owned by individuals (known as industrialists). They decide what will be produced, in what quantities and specifications, the place and time of production, the process to be used, the workers to be employed etc. Unfortunately, some of their decisions carry a certain degree of risk as to the possible outcome. It is uncertain whether the goods to be produced will satisfy the market in terms of quality and price (other producers may offer better products for the same price, or products of the same quality at lower prices). Because of the risks taken, the industrialists charge their customers with prices well above their costs. Besides, in a market economy the aim of producers is to increase their own wealth (i.e. make profits). Consequently, all private industrial investment is channelled to the areas where the expected rate of profit is higher, or less uncertain.

Profits and Losses

Knowledge is a valuable friend

The principal aim of private enterprise is profit maximization (i.e. the maximum possible increase in the value of the owners' equity). The entrepreneurs take the most important decisions regarding business operations, and expect a return on the capital employed that will compensate them for the time spent on the project. Unfortunately, some of the decisions taken are based on certain assumptions about the future, for some production is carried out in anticipation of demand. Economic miscalculations or unexpected political, commercial, industrial or technological developments may turn an apparently profitable investment into a financial disaster. For the risks involved, the entrepreneurs will not proceed with an investment unless the expected rate of return on capital employed exceeds that of the best alternative business opportunity that carries the same degree of risk. The higher the risks involved in a capital venture the higher the profits required by potential investors.

In a market economy most private capital investments are gambles. But the experienced entrepreneur as a professional gambler knows that fortune usually sides first with the fresh players and then with the richest or most experienced. Money and knowledge have a tendency to accumulate!

Poverty and Wages

The power of money lies in our deficiencies

The aim of industrial production is to make certain things more useful to mankind by changing their form and substance through various processes (e.g. make paper and boats from forest trees, detergents from chemical compounds etc). Industrial production, by definition, is not a natural process. It is a process developed by men, performed by men and directed by men. The first stage calls for scientific work, the second for labour and the third for managerial work. All stages are interrelated and interdependent and call for the expenditure of human energy. But the energy expended can only be replenished by an extra consumption of food, and the time spent by a greater enjoyment of leisure. This calls for a reward which raises the standard of living of the participants (each of them presumably an expert in his own field). But one's standard of living depends both on current and accumulated income (i.e. savings). The latter may have remained in a liquid form (e.g. bank deposits), or turned into real property (e.g. a house). Consequently, it is not current income itself an incentive to work but its marginal value to the participants. Thus, an income of $ 100,000 p.a is a strong incentive to work for most people but a waste of time for a multi-millionaire. On the other hand, the poorer the workers the higher the marginal value of their wages. The higher the marginal value of their wages the greater their satisfaction from their contract of employment. The greater their satisfaction from their contract of employment the greater their commitment to the objectives of their employers. The greater their commitment to the objectives of their employers the greater their efforts at work. The greater their efforts at work the higher their productivity (provided that they are competent). The higher their productivity the greater the volume of goods produced per man employed. The greater the volume of goods produced the higher the income from sales (provided that market prices remain stable and the demand strong). The higher the income from sales the greater the profits to be made. In conclusion, the poorer the workers the greater the profits to be made.

Bearing in mind that the financial position of most workers is relatively weak, it is inevitable that prolonged conditions of unemployment will compel a considerable part of the labour force to live on their savings until they fall below the poverty line (i.e. become very poor). Subsequently, labour unemployment gives a boost to business profits. The workers in the long run remain poor while the rich businessmen become richer and richer. This is a serious flaw of the market economy.

Profits versus Wages

Getting rich is not a charitable engagement

The reward of the participants in an enterprise also depends on their legal relations with the land used and the capital employed in the business. Property titles on the land used and the capital employed give special rewards to their holders. While ordinary workers receive a fixed reward per hour employed irrespective of their individual contribution in production, the business owners have a claim on the profits made by the enterprise; the greater the profits the higher their reward. Wages, on the other hand, are considered as an expense of the enterprise and for that reason the higher the wages the lower the profits (provided that productivity does not rise there upon) and vice versa. As a result, there is a conflict of interest between workers on one side and business owners on the other as to the amount of wages to be paid and the amount of labour to be exerted.

In the ordinary course of business, the workers do not associate their wages and salaries with the profits earned. So long as they are satisfied with their pay-roll and working conditions, they use all their power for the benefit of the enterprise. Subsequently, their productivity will remain high over time and may even increase. Unfortunately, profitability is not only a matter of productivity and wage levels. It is a matter of relative costs in general as compared to sales revenues. Transport and energy costs are affected by the location of the business so that some producers have cheaper access to supply sources or the consumers' market than others. The quality of goods produced, however, must not be underestimated. The demand for goods of high quality remains strong even in recession.

The entrepreneurs in an attempt to increase their profit margins sometimes combine together and raise prices without increasing the level of wages. That rise in prices brings about a fall in the value of money and wages. Then industrial unrest and action may follow until real wages are restored to their former levels. Most of the strikes in the 1970's worldwide where chain reactions to the price increases triggered off by the oil cartel and certain industrial giants.

Technology, Productivity, Profits and Unemployment

Unemployment is the canker of our society

The aim of technology is to increase the volume of production per worker (i.e. raise productivity). The use of modern technology at work in the last 200 years added enormously to the quantity and quality of goods produced per worker worldwide. The gains from the rise in productivity, however, have not been equally distributed. In fact, the owners of the technological equipment took the lion's share and the workers who had no property rights very little. When the increased amount of goods produced was sold without reductions in selling prices, there was an increase in profits as a result of the increase in the revenue from sales. When the extra production could not be sold at former prices, there was a pressure for a reduction in the number of workers employed. Thus, the increases in productivity were accompanied by increases in profits and unemployment.

After 1980 we have seen a global trend for a simultaneous increase in corporate profits and for a reduction in the number of workers employed by industrialists. Economists so far have failed to develop socially acceptable plans for the elimination of unemployment and underemployment (the employment of workers at jobs inferior to their profession, e.g. an engineer working as a taxi-driver). An acceptable plan would be one that continuously reduces unemployment without reducing personal incomes or the quality of goods produced.

Production, Consumption, Savings and Investment

It is much easier to make the rich richer than the poor rich

Despite the amount of goods currently produced worldwide, there is still a want for proper food, clothes and accommodation by a large proportion of the population in most countries. Even in advanced economies such as Britain, U.S.A., Germany and Japan more than 30% of the population are not satisfied with their daily menu and current dwelling. Unfortunately, the world production does not provide for all men. Besides, the level of consumption varies according to private incomes and wealth. Consequently, the people lying below the poverty line can barely survive throughout the year.

Long-term benefits usually call for short-term sacrifices. Thus, the entrepreneurs in an endeavour to increase productivity and efficiency often invest in modern technology. This implies a transfer of resources from the production of consumer goods to the production of industrial capital. But the producers of capital goods must be fed and taken care of. This calls for the formation of resources in consumer goods to be used by capital producers. The above resources in a market economy are in the form of commercial capital. In fact, the production of industrial capital under private enterprise is impossible without the previous growth of commercial capital, which is an accumulation of wealth in the form of commodities. This presumes a surplus of production over consumption (i.e. the existence and growth of savings).

Private savings and investments usually go hand in hand. However, there are times when they do not proceed with the same speed. When investments lag behind savings for long, unemployment tends to rise until investments catch up. Then employment is restored to former levels.

Wages, Profits, Interest
Rates and Investments

The truth is an idea that corresponds to reality

The aim of industrial investments is to increase labour productivity (i.e. the output per worker employed). On the other hand, the principal aim of private enterprise is to increase the owners' equity (the value of their property). Consequently, private industrial investments are only plausible when they add to the profits of a business.

Since industrial capital operates as a substitute for labour, the higher the level of wages the more the opportunities for profitable industrial investments. Similarly, the lower the interest rates the lower the cost of financial capital and the higher the returns on borrowed funds. Thus, private industrial investments are fuelled by reductions in interest rates and increases in wages!

Countries with relatively high wage levels are more likely to use labour saving devices (i.e. capital goods) whereas low wages make real investments in capital industries more profitable (industries producing capital goods for world markets). The postwar economic development of Germany and Japan was based on the growth of such industries.

The Role of Banks

Happiness is a matter of balance

The banks borrow funds from money holders in the form of deposits and lend them to companies and individuals at a much higher rate of interest. The rate of interest paid on deposits primarily depends on their period, the current rate of inflation and the demand for loans, whereas the rate of interest charged also depends on the calculated risk of the investment and the security provided. In fact, the banks act as intermediaries between creditors (i.e. bank depositors etc) and debtors. In this respect, they help to maintain an equilibrium between savings and investments on an international scale. This is indispensable for economic growth and monetary stability in market economies. When the demand for loans exceeds the supply of savings there is a tendency for interest rates to rise. On the other hand, when the supply of savings exceeds the demand for loans there is a tendency for interest rates to fall, as the banks have no reason to pay interest rates higher than those required to maintain the necessary amount of deposits.

After the Second World War, the big banks acting together can lend money which they do not own or owe (i.e produce money from nothing!) as long as they all expand at the same rate (so that their balances with the central bank are not seriously affected). This financial privilege of the banks is unique in private enterprise and gives them a considerable advantage over all other business not only at times of economic expansion but also of contraction. Thus, business competition in private enterprise is actually not fair not only between businesses of the same trade but also between banks and non-financial firms.

The Role of the Stock Market

Lover of money, servant of wealth

Before the Industrial Revolution certain business ventures were not carried out because the participants were not willing to risk the whole of their property for any amount of profit whatsoever. The need for a limited liability on the part of investors led business lawyers to the creation of the joint stock company, a legal entity separate from its members (owners). The capital required for a business venture was determined in advance and provided by investors in various proportions in return for shares issued. Through the joint stock company the liability of the business owners was limited to the amount of capital so raised. Each share represented a definite fraction of the total equity capital of the company. The company itself had an existence of its own and was not affected by regular changes in share ownership. During the Industrial Revolution it became the principal form of big business and the instrument for the growth and development of capital markets.

The need to raise venture capital, and to realize business investments at will without jeopardizing the relevant enterprises, led to the establishment of suitable locations where the investors could meet in person, or via their agents (stock brokers), and negotiate the company shares. The above locations became known as stock exchanges and the markets so formed as stock markets.

The price of an ordinary share of a company listed on the stock exchange represents a fraction of the current value of the expected profits to be made by the particular company in the near future. Since they are based on personal estimates about the future, ordinary share prices on the stock exchange may fluctuate widely even during a single day. For that reason, the ordinary shares traded in the stock markets are the most favourable objects for speculation by investors who want to make big profits fast even at a great risk.

The Role of Money in a Market Economy

Money is the blood of capitalism

Today, more than 90% of world money is in the form of bank deposits and notes in circulation. They have no intrinsic value at all; their value lies in their universal acceptance as mediums of exchange. In that capacity they can be used for the settlement of trade debts, and subsequently for all forms of debt.

The value of the monetary unit is affected by changes in the supply of money and goods. A large increase in the total stock of money, ceteris paribus, will soon bring down the value of its unit (i.e. bring about a rise in prices). On the other hand, a large increase in the volume of national production, ceteris paribus, will soon bring down commodity prices thereby increasing the value of the monetary unit.

In its capacity as a medium of exchange money is used for rewarding the owners and producers of wealth for the goods supplied and the services provided. In a market economy the supply of goods and the provision of services is matched by the circulation of money in the opposite direction. The possession of money becomes a condition for most material benefits, and consequently its distribution assumes paramount importance. The people with a few material possessions and little money (i.e. the poor) cannot survive long without a job, whereas the holders of large amounts of money can enjoy a high life style without working. In this case, money serves as a store of values to be used in the future. An accumulation of money, therefore, may also be used as capital (for the purchase of commodities, hiring labour etc).

Money used as capital becomes a source of income to its holders and investors. Interest accrues on money lent to profitable business enterprises, and dividends are paid to shareholders for the capital vested. While most goods have a tendency to disintegrate and decline with time, money, on the contrary, has a tendency to accumulate and advance!

The Role of the State

A society without welfare is a family without affection

The state, like the limited liability company, is a human invention. From the legal point of view, it stands like a national company. It employs people to perform certain tasks, and enters into contracts like any other legal person. It is usually run by a board of directors, known as the national government, presumably in the interests of the nation.

The modern state is a descendant of the ancient kingdom. It extends over large parts of land which are protected by armed men (the Armed Forces, the Police etc). It presumably operates for the promotion of the interests of its members (known as citizens) like any other public company. Its authority, however, is much more extensive. The state may interfere in all aspects of life presumably to protect the interests of society as a whole. It may enforce legislation to affect the terms of trade and employment, the conditions for property transfers, the extent of civil liberties etc. in spite of private opposition. In this respect it is a political organisation rather than a financial one.

The subjects (or citizens) who are permanent employees of the state are known as civil servants. They are paid from the subscriptions collected from its members, known as taxes, which may also be used for financing wars, public works etc. In addition, the proceeds from taxation may be used in order to improve the financial position of the poor, to reduce unemployment, to promote public education, to encourage cultural development, to protect public health etc.

A state may take the form of a kingdom or a republic (usually a democracy). The ultimate authority in a kingdom is hereditary (it passes from parent to child, from the king or queen to a prince or princess). In a democracy, however, the ultimate authority rests with the people. They choose their representatives in Parliament for a limited period of time and for a specific purpose (through regularly held national elections and for implementing a definite political programme). A monarchy obviously demonstrates a greater concentration of political and financial power than a democracy.

In respect of planning, organization and direction a democratic state resembles a public liability company (i.e. a Wall Street giant). The Parliament or Congress acts as the assembly of large shareholders whereas the government acts as the board of directors. With respect to internal control, however, a democratic state lags behind a private company although it excels in social and environmental issues.

The Transfer of Property Rights

Succession is the mother of class society

It is self-evident that any transfer of property rights is for the benefit of the transferee and against the interests of the transferor. In the eyes of the law the transferee takes the position of the transferor, who surrenders his claims on the property concerned. For that reason, in the ordinary course of business there is always a two-way transfer of property rights (i.e. an exchange of rights). In case of love, however, some transfers are without consideration (i.e. one way transfers); the property rights are not "gained" but conferred as gifts or bequests. As a result, a large number of people, nowadays, enjoy vast property rights for no consideration at all!

Private property is not a natural right but a social concession. The rules governing private ownership are formulated by society as a whole and are deemed to further its long-term interests. The rules are deemed to raise the standard of living of the whole population by promoting the production of wealth and ensuring its equitable distribution. They should also help to combat poverty and unemployment, offer universal educational and vocational opportunities, improve productivity and workmanship, protect public health etc.

Some of the above targets of public policy may be presented as lying in opposite directions. For instance, the protection of public health and the environment may seem to call for measures that discourage industrial development, labour employment and economic prosperity. Similarly, high income taxation may seem to discourage improvements in productivity. The truth, however, is quite different. The position of the targets must be considered in relation to the standing of the policy makers. The aim is not to make everybody happier than before, as some people are already happy enough. The aim is to efface human misery. But in societies ruled by money and not by virtue the interests of the rich lay supreme.

The state may intervene in the transfer of property rights through taxation. In a market economy the exchange value of property is reduced by the amount of the tax imposed on each transfer (indirect taxation). In such cases the transferor may ask for a higher price, the increase depending on the financial position of the transferee. This is equivalent to a reduction in the value of money, which is more painful to the poor because it reduces still further the amount of goods they can afford to buy. Direct taxation, on the other hand, reduces the value of personal incomes, usually on a progressive scale. As a result, direct taxation is usually against the interests of the rich, whereas indirect taxation is generally against the interests of the poor. In this respect, it appears that taxation is against the interests of the people in general and for the benefit of the politicians and the civil servants. But one has first to consider what one pays in taxes and what one receives in the form of social security, public education, road construction, environmental protection etc.

Despite taxation, certain property rights are not diminished by transfer. Bank notes and bank deposits, and bearer shares and debentures may be transferred from one person to another undetected by the Inland Revenue. As a matter of fact, it is possible for a multi-millionaire to transfer a large part of his personal property to his children without paying any taxes at all! On paper, the richer you are the more taxes you pay, but in practice there are certain ways to evade the Inland Revenue, as current legislation does not provide for the guard of certain escape routes, all of them common property of the very rich. Besides, no politician would have a good chance of becoming a legislator without the support of the millionaires if he were to pass effective legislation on income taxation and legacies; no wonder for the incurable budget deficits!

The Current Accumulation
of Property Rights

*The uneven distribution of money and wealth
leads a few people to paradise and a lot to hell*

Except for Russia, Cuba and China, about 50% of world industrial production is currently produced by 100 multinational companies. They are all based in the most advanced industrial countries (U.S.A., England, Germany, Japan, France, Italy, Holland) and each of them is controlled and directed by no more than 10 families. In summary, about 1000 families control and direct industrial production all over the world (with the exception of Russia, Cuba and China) leaving small detail and work to local industrialists. The families have absolute control over scientific discoveries, and take advantage of current inventions and innovations. They use the most sophisticated equipment in production and management. They have immediate access to all the major political and financial centres of the world, as they own the major T.V. stations, the popular press (including book publishers), film producers, banks, stock brokers etc. Moreover, they do not have to worry much about legislation as the most prominent politicians in all the major political parties are either confidants or obliging servants. Last but not least, they pay very little in income taxes, or estate duties, as they control their financial empires through holding companies based on "tax heaven" states, where they channel the largest part of the profits made by their subsidiaries by under pricing their exports to their parent company and providing her with interest free trade credits.

Since they can transfer vast sums of money from one country to another with a simple phone call, they can exert strong pressure on currency rates and thereby support or undermine the monetary policies of national governments accordingly. Thus, sterling came under great pressure in the early 1976 when Harold Wilson was following policies contrary to their interests.

The accumulation of such power in the hands of a few thousand, most of them completely unknown to the general public, undermines the very foundations of democracy in all countries and societies, for democracy is based on the cardinal principle that all citizens can exert the same amount of influence on their governments (one man, one vote). Despite the ostensible equality, the billionaires are not only absolute masters of huge estates but also shadow directors of governments, as they can check the long term economic growth of unruly states by blockading their access to world markets for foreign capital, strategic commodities and advanced technological equipment. This has devastating effects on the lives of millions of people who occasionally dare to vote for insubordinate governments.

Society in a Market Economy

Nothing against society may be just or right

Every society as a whole functions without regard to the will of any single member (no king can rule over his subjects without some popular consent). Nevertheless, from time to time certain individuals in dominant positions lay down the rules of conduct that regulate public life and business activity (i.e. a constitution). In the end, a set of laws will regulate all aspects of life until the population decides for a different system. Thus, in 1789 the French people revolted against the feudal system with the view to establish a democracy, whereas in 1917 the Russian people revolted against the tsar and his court to establish a socialist state. Both revolutions imposed severe restrictions on hereditary rights. Political rights were detached from property rights while all large real estates were confiscated (became public property). In the eyes of the law, all people became equal irrespective of their social background, occupation, education or financial position.

It has already become common property that the rights of people are determined by the relative strength of social groups with competing interests. In democratic societies the political rights are equally distributed (one man, one vote). Equality, however, is not extended to property rights. The distribution of property rights is left on the operation of market forces rather than on social considerations. Even today, more than 200 years after the French Revolution, most people in France and many other countries are born and die either rich or poor no matter what they offer or take from society. More specifically, the richest 5% of the population in the capitalist world can live in luxury and die even richer without working at all, while the poorest 30% will live in misery and die poor despite their hard work. In fact, social inequality is still as great as before the French Revolution, the difference lying in the form of accumulated property. Before the French Revolution it was in the form of real estate, nowadays is in the form of company shares.

The Road to a Less Autocratic and More Prosperous Society

Quality is a matter of quantitative relationships

The secrecy demanded by law on bank deposit holdings and transactions and the existence of bearer shares make it possible for the rich financiers to transfer the largest part of their property to their children without paying any taxes at all. Thus, the largest part of property rights is transferred from father to son without consideration and is equivalent to the class system that existed before the French Revolution, when the largest part of private wealth was not acquired by personal work but was just inherited. This perpetuity is contrary to the spirit of the French Revolution and undermines the very foundations of democracy ("all people are born with equal rights", "equal opportunities for all"). Therefore, it is imperative for the advancement of democracy to pass and enforce legislation that seriously restricts the transfer of property rights without true consideration (i.e. by gift or inheritance). For those who may claim that this interferes with the free will of the property owners it is necessary to repeat that "private property is not a natural gift but a concession by society to the hard working individuals". Undoubtedly, it is in the interests of society to provide children with the means for a better life (i.e. a house) but not the means to lead a whole life in luxury without working. Drones in control of immense wealth are not only unnecessary but also socially dangerous. (One must not identify position of employment with actual work performed; some kings reigned but never ruled themselves). Therefore, to place a ceiling on the value of property transferred without true consideration is more than just. Besides, it follows the spirit of the French Revolution.

A ceiling at $ 10.000.000 is more than enough for the industrious man who happens to be the son of a multi-millionaire. In the absence of children and grandchildren, a ceiling at $ 1.000.000 for nephews and nieces is a good bonanza. On the other hand, there must be a floor for children before any estate duties are paid. This floor may well stand as high as $ 100.000 (i.e. for an estate of a smaller value no duties to be paid). Above that floor (applicable only to widows and children) there must be a progressive duty rate starting from 30% and ending at 70% as on Table I.

A ceiling at $ 10.000.000 will affect no more than a few thousand families in each country (less than 1o/oo of the world population). That is necessary for the establishment and preservation of a true democracy. Besides, every citizen must contribute to the expenses of the state in accordance with his current income and estate. For that reason, income tax should not apply to incomes below the minimum wage level.

Income tax may well start from the above level at the rate of 10% and end up at 40% for high incomes (i.e. progressive taxation) as on Table II (not applicable to legal persons).

TABLE I

VALUE OF PROPERTY BEFORE TAXATION			DUTY RATE APPLICABLE	SUCCESSION DUTY PAYABLE		VALUE OF PROPERTY AFTER TAXATION	
$				$		$	
1	-	100.000	0%	0		AS BEFORE	
100.001	-	150.000	30%	UP TO	15.000	UP TO	135.000
150.001	-	200.000	32%	UP TO	31.000	UP TO	169.000
200.001	-	250.000	34%	UP TO	48.000	UP TO	202.000
250.001	-	300.000	36%	UP TO	66.000	UP TO	234.000
300.001	-	350.000	38%	UP TO	85.000	UP TO	265.000
350.001	-	400.000	40%	UP TO	105.000	UP TO	295.000
400.001	-	450.000	42%	UP TO	126.000	UP TO	324.000
450.001	-	500.000	44%	UP TO	148.000	UP TO	352.000
500.001	-	550.000	46%	UP TO	171.000	UP TO	379.000
550.001	-	600.000	48%	UP TO	195.000	UP TO	405.000
600.001	-	650.000	50%	UP TO	220.000	UP TO	430.000
650.001	-	700.000	52%	UP TO	246.000	UP TO	454.000
700.001	-	750.000	54%	UP TO	273.000	UP TO	477.000
750.001	-	800.000	56%	UP TO	301.000	UP TO	499.000
800.001	-	850.000	58%	UP TO	330.000	UP TO	520.000
850.001	-	900.000	60%	UP TO	360.000	UP TO	540.000
900.001	-	950.000	62%	UP TO	391.000	UP TO	559.000
950.001	-	1.000.000	64%	UP TO	423.000	UP TO	577.000
1.000.001	-	1.050.000	66%	UP TO	456.000	UP TO	594.000
1.050.001	-	1.100.000	68%	UP TO	490.000	UP TO	610.000
OVER		1.100.000	70%	OVER	490.000	OVER	610.000
....				....		....	
FOR		2.000.000			1.120.000		880.000
FOR		2.400.000			1.400.000		1.000.000
FOR		32.400.000			22.400.000		10.000.000
OVER		32.400.000		OVER	22.400.000	ONLY(!)	10.000.000

TABLE II

ANNUAL INCOME BEFORE TAXATION			TAX RATE APPLICABLE	TAX PAYABLE		INCOME AFTER TAXATION	
US $				US $		US $	
1	-	10.000	0%	0		AS BEFORE	
10.000	-	12.000	10%	UP TO	200	UP TO	11.800
12.000	-	14.000	12%	UP TO	440	UP TO	13.560
14.000	-	16.000	14%	UP TO	720	UP TO	15.280
16.000	-	18.000	16%	UP TO	1.040	UP TO	16.960
18.000	-	20.000	18%	UP TO	1.400	UP TO	18.600
20.000	-	22.000	20%	UP TO	1.800	UP TO	20.200
22.000	-	24.000	22%	UP TO	2.240	UP TO	21.760
24.000	-	26.000	24%	UP TO	2.720	UP TO	23.280
26.000	-	28.000	26%	UP TO	3.240	UP TO	24.760
28.000	-	30.000	28%	UP TO	3.800	UP TO	26.200
30.000	-	32.000	30%	UP TO	4.400	UP TO	27.600
32.000	-	34.000	32%	UP TO	5.040	UP TO	28.960
34.000	-	36.000	34%	UP TO	5.720	UP TO	30.280
36.000	-	38.000	36%	UP TO	6.440	UP TO	31.560
38.000	-	40.000	38%	UP TO	7.200	UP TO	32.800
OVER	-	40.000	40%	OVER	7.200	OVER	32.800
....				....		....	
FOR		50.000			11.200		38.800
FOR		60.000			15.200		44.800
FOR		70.000			19.200		50.800
FOR		80.000			23.200		56.800
FOR		90.000			27.200		62.800
FOR		100.000			31.200		68.800
FOR		200.000			71.200		128.800
FOR		300.000			111.200		188.800
FOR		400.000			151.200		248.800
FOR		500000			191.200		308.800
FOR		1.000.000			391.200		608.800

Table II applies to annual incomes from personal work (i.e. wages, salaries and fees). For that reason, even for high incomes tax rates should not exceed 40%, for they might become a strong disincentive to work. In the case of incomes from investments, however, higher tax rates should not be excluded in certain circumstances. Thus, a 30% tax to apply on the normal profits of firms and companies. In addition, a 70% tax to apply on their super-profits (i.e. profits above normal) as follows:

For the industrial and financial sector of the economy (i.e. manufacturing companies, banks etc) as super-profits to be considered those exceeding 50% of the sum total of labour expenses and the book value of the technological equipment used (i.e. plant and machinery, computers etc) as it appears on the relative balance sheet at the end of the year (wages over $ 1.000 p.w. and salaries over $ 100.000 p.a. to be excluded from calculation). Thus, a technologically advanced industrial corporation paying $ 10 million on wages and salaries (as shown on the profit and loss account for the relevant year) with a book value of capital equipment standing at $ 30 million would be taxed for profits less than $ 20 million (normal profits) at the rate of 30% (e.g. for a profit of $ 20 million would have to pay $ 6 million in taxes). However, if the same corporation had made a profit of $ 30 million it would have to pay $ 13 million in taxes ($ 6 m on normal profits and $ 7 m on super-profits).

For taxation purposes, firms and companies to make provisions for depreciation using the Reducing Balance Method as follows:

ASSET	DEPRECIATION RATE
Premises	7%
Plant and Machinery	20%
Computers	40%

For the commercial sector as super profits to be considered those exceeding 5% of the sales revenue of the wholesalers and 10% of the retailers. Thus, a merchant exporting agricultural products with annual sales at $ 200 million would not be allowed to declare net profits over $ 10 million as being normal (In case of a strong export demand, this super-profits tax system would induce export traders to share part of their super-profits with the domestic producers, who would be thus encouraged to increase production and employment. Similarly, a strong domestic demand for imports would be met by an increase in their volume rather than an increase in their prices, a cause of inflation).

The super-profits tax system encourages industrial investments and discourages unjustified price increases. Therefore, it is not only a strong channel of surplus funds to the Inland Revenue but also a powerful weapon against technological obsolescence and inflation. Nevertheless, it should not apply to net profits less than $ 1.000.000 per annum.

The distribution of company profits must not precede the payment of taxes. No dividends should be paid before full payment of the monies due to the Inland Revenue and the local authorities is effected. The 15% tax levied on the interest paid to bank deposits should be extended to the dividends paid to company shareholders. Apart from those taxes, no other taxes should be paid with regard to the income received in the form of dividends or interest. A 5% tax should also be levied on rent paid. This should be part of a special tax levied on rent received from property let, as on Table III (calculated separately from other sources).

For the purpose of fair taxation, all property of substantial value should be declared to the Inland Revenue (i.e. real estate, company shares and debentures, government bonds, bank deposits etc) and recorded in data banks with the help of advanced computers. An extensive use of the existing networks for data transfers would enable the Inland Revenue to have a complete and up to date record of private incomes and estates. This necessitates the full cooperation of banks and companies. In such a case the above programme would help combat not only tax evasion but also drug trade, which is facilitated by money laundering.

TABLE III

TOTAL ANNUAL RENTAL BEFORE TAXATION			TAX RATE APPLICABLE	TAX PAYABLE		TOTAL ANNUAL RENTAL AFTER TAXATION	
US $				US $		US $	
1	-	12.000	5%	UP TO	600	UP TO	11.400
12.000	-	14.000	6%	UP TO	720	UP TO	13.280
14.000	-	16.000	7%	UP TO	860	UP TO	15.140
16.000	-	18.000	8%	UP TO	1.020	UP TO	16.980
18.000	-	20.000	9%	UP TO	1.200	UP TO	18.800
20.000	-	22.000	10%	UP TO	1.400	UP TO	20.600
22.000	-	24.000	11%	UP TO	1.620	UP TO	22.380
24.000	-	26.000	12%	UP TO	1.860	UP TO	24.140
26.000	-	28.000	13%	UP TO	2.120	UP TO	25.880
28.000	-	30.000	14%	UP TO	2.400	UP TO	27.600
30.000	-	32.000	15%	UP TO	2.700	UP TO	29.300
32.000	-	34.000	16%	UP TO	3.020	UP TO	30.980
34.000	-	36.000	17%	UP TO	3.360	UP TO	32.640
36.000	-	38.000	18%	UP TO	3.720	UP TO	34.280
38.000	-	40.000	19%	UP TO	4.100	UP TO	35.900
OVER	-	40.000	20%	OVER	4.100	OVER	35.900
....				....		....	
FOR		50.000			6.100		43.900
FOR		60.000			8.100		51.900
FOR		70.000			10.100		59.900
FOR		80.000			12.100		67.900
FOR		90.000			14.100		75.900
FOR		100.000			16.100		83.900
FOR		200.000			36.100		163.900
FOR		300.000			56.100		243.900
FOR		400.000			76.100		323.900
FOR		500.000			96.100		403.900
FOR		1.000.000			196.100		803.900

TABLE IV

VALUE OF PRIVATE PROPERTY BEFORE TAXATION			TAX RATE APPLICABLE	TAX PAYABLE		VALUE OF PROPERTY AFTER TAXATION	
		$			$		$
1	-	1.000.000	0%		0		SAME AS BEFORE
1.000.001	-	2.000.000	1.1%	UP TO	11.000	UP TO	1.989.000
2.000.001	-	3.000.000	1.2%	UP TO	23.000	UP TO	2.977.000
3.000.001	-	4.000.000	1.3%	UP TO	36.000	UP TO	3.964.000
4.000.001	-	5.000.000	1.4%	UP TO	50.000	UP TO	4.950.000
5.000.001	-	6.000.000	1.5%	UP TO	65.000	UP TO	5.935.000
6.000.001	-	7.000.000	1.6%	UP TO	81.000	UP TO	6.919.000
7.000.001	-	8.000.000	1.7%	UP TO	98.000	UP TO	7.902.000
8.000.001	-	9.000.000	1.8%	UP TO	116.000	UP TO	8.884.000
9.000.001	-	10.000.000	1.9%	UP TO	135.000	UP TO	9.865.000
OVER	-	10.000.000	2%	OVER	135.000	OVER	9.865.000
....				....		....	
FOR		20.000.000			335.000		19.665.000
FOR		30.000.000			535.000		29.465.000
FOR		40.000.000			735.000		39.265.000
FOR		50.000.000			935.000		49.065.000
FOR		100.000.000			1.935.000		98.065.000

Once the ultimate owners of all real and financial assets have been identified, a progressive property tax should be levied on all private estates totalling over $ 1.000.000 (adding in all real and personal property) as on Table IV (not applicable to legal persons).

While direct taxation is used in order to improve the existing social conditions and support the current economic activity, indirect taxation may be used for the protection of domestic production against foreign competition. However, the most important reason for imposing a consumption tax is to divert production and consumption from uses that contribute least to personal and social welfare. Besides, the government has a duty to protect the public from industrial pollution, as most goods are still produced by processes burdening the environment. Despite many efforts, the extraction of minerals is still a cause of environmental destruction, and the chemical industries a source of earth pollution. The use of power stations adds to air pollution. Oil wells and refineries add to water pollution. In summary, most industrial production and waste are sources of environmental destruction or contamination. For that reason, the price of goods produced must also reflect those costs; the higher the environmental costs the higher the tax rates that should be imposed. Thus, a tax on tobacco must carry the highest possible rate, as smoking is not only the main cause of death for smokers but also the main source of air pollution in public places such as bars, restaurants, discos, conference halls and transport stations. Human life, in general, cannot be disconnected from external developments, for any environmental disturbance bears upon our lives. The same applies to social disturbances. In this respect, and for the protection of public health and life, alcoholic drinks such as brandy, whisky, gin and vodca (i.e. "high spirits") must be heavily taxed, for the excessive use of alcohol leads to a loss of self-control and balance, impotence, inability to work properly and efficiently, to traffic accidents and death. Nobody knows better the hazards of over-consumption than the children of heavy drinkers and smokers.

The interests of third parties, therefore, must also be taken into account. The long term interests of society as a whole must not be set aside by individuals who live for the spark of the moment. At this point, it is necessary to state explicitly the principles on which all the suggestions have been based.

First, the long-term interests of mankind to predominate over any short-term benefits.

Second, the interests of humanity to prevail over the interests of any particular society or group of individuals.

Third, everybody as an individual by the end of his life to have made some net contribution to society (i.e. the total value of his personal work to exceed the total value of the goods he consumed during his lifetime).

If the first principle had been followed by all producers, large parts of the Earth would not have become so unfit for human life. The destruction of natural habitat in the name of industrial development seriously reduces the vital space for man.

If the second principle had been followed by all nations and social groups, there would have been no wars among the people. Both World Wars, which resulted in the loss of 100 million people, broken families, widespread destruction and misery, were bloody violations of the second principle.

If everybody were to follow the third principle, our society would have no pests, thieves and robbers, beggars and drones; it would be a just and prosperous society without the present poverty and crime, as everybody would have the opportunity to participate in the production process to the best of his abilities and also have the will to share the fruits of labour with his fellow workers and citizens.

It is very unlikely that the above principles will ever be accepted and followed by the established interests of today's world. One must be naive to expect that the people who are mainly responsible for social inequality and environmental pollution and destruction will ever accept and support political principles that suggest policies adverse to their own interests and private pursuits. They do not care about the hundreds of millions who live in miserable conditions, despite their hard work, wondering if hell is not only for the bad but also for those born poor, for the unlucky. It seems after all that Paradise and Hell are for the living, not for the dead!

Undoutedly, it would be in the interests of mankind if prices reflected not only the costs of production and distribution to the producers and traders but also social costs such as environmental pollution and destruction, public health reduction, hooliganism, accident proneness etc. Those costs should be added to the costs of production and distribution. In this respect the current taxation system provides an appropriate framework. The social costs could be allotted to the respective products through the V.A.T. (Value Added Tax), a sales tax collected in instalments at each stage of the production and distribution process. Thus, considering the contribution (positive or negative) of each product towards public health promotion and preservation, a tax rate scale could be devised with the help of a committee of scientists such as physicists, chemists, geologists and doctors in order to discourage the production and consumption of certain goods.

For products like fresh fruit, vegetables, and sea food no V.A.T. should be imposed. For canned food, ordinary clothes and shoes an 8% rate seems reasonable. For household appliances, electronics and ordinary cars 18% is fair enough. For bottled wine and beer 36% is more than adequate. For high-speed cars, private helicopters and airplanes 48% is not much. For tobacco and strong drinks like whisky, gin, brandy and vodca a 72% rate to discourage over consumption. In addition, a special tax should be imposed on products responsible for extensive environmental pollution and damage like petrol and plastic (literally speaking their producers and users are responsible for that and not the products themselves).

Certain governments impose high V.A.T. rates for luxuries such as racing boats, sports-cars, furs and expensive jewellery on the presumption that such products are used by high income groups for reasons of prestige rather. A Value Added Tax may also be imposed on the services provided by electricians, plumbers, doctors, solicitors etc. In such cases the ordinary V.A.T. rate (i.e. 18%) seems most appropriate, and serves as a supplementary tax to income tax.

Taxation is just one side of the fiscal policy; the other side is public expenditure. The difference between public revenues and expenditures leads to a budget deficit or surplus (a short-fall of public revenues over public expenditures leads to a budget deficit). A relatively small budget deficit is not bad for the economy. In fact, at times of high unemployment a budget deficit provides extra income and jobs that would have been lost under a balanced budget.

Public expenditure must be planned very carefully. Every dollar spent by the government must be beneficial not only to the recipient concerned but also to the society as a whole. Fiscal policy becomes meaningful only when it promotes economic and cultural development and raises the standard of living of the whole population. It does not serve society if it perpetuates the existing socioeconomic inequalities or fails to provide for the sick, the old and the unemployed. Medical care, education, employment and pension should be universal rights. Nevertheless, part of the cost of special medical treatment and advanced education should be born by the beneficiaries themselves, the amount depending on their financial position.

Despite the post war economic growth worldwide, public expenditure on health and education is in most countries still insufficient while at the same time billions of dollars are spent on "defence". Those billions are often described as "the price of freedom" but in fact they usually are a price for the preservation of the existing social class structure in each country, which may be threatened by social or economic developments in neighbouring states. The world is in need of healthy, intelligent and educated people who live and work in peace and not of "smart bombs" that kill or cripple people in other societies when they are not willing to place our interests above their own.

While fiscal policy directly affects private incomes and social benefits, business activity and prosperity are also affected by changes in the supply, value and cost of money. The policies aimed at controlling or effecting such changes are known as monetary policies. Thus, monetary policy is concerned with the growth of bank deposits, the circulation of cash, the rate of inflation and the level of interest rates.

The rate of inflation must be kept as low as possible. Inflation rates over 20% per annum are difficult to control. An inflation rate over 100% p.a. may soon lead to a hyper inflation, an accelerating fall in the value of money that can only be checked by a change in the monetary base (i.e. the introduction of a new currency to take the place of the old with a value compatible with the world strong currencies). This remedy for hyper inflation was first used by the German monetary authorities in the early 1920's and proved quite successful. The same remedy should also be used by the Russians in order to attain monetary stability before the year 2000. (In most cases, hyper inflation is the result of a failure of the banking system to absorb the extra liquidity produced by a series of large budget deficits. For that reason, a reduction in budget deficits must be accompanied by a reorganisation of the whole banking system if inflation is to be reduced to an acceptable rate).

The success or failure of a monetary policy largely depends on the level of interest rates (nominal[1] and real[2]). In the long-term, real interest rates should be around 2% p.a.

1.nominal interest rates are the interest rates as they appear on public records for financial transactions (interst paid on deposits, charged for loans etc.)
2.real interest rates are fictional rates indicating the real cost of borrowed funds (real interest rates=nominal interest rates-inflation rate).

If they are below 1% p.a. they provide no real incentive for savings. On the other hand, if they rise above 3% p.a. they increase the cost of credit to a level that discourages firms and companies to borrow funds for investments. Thus, in the first case we have an excessive liquidity in the economy which will soon lead to higher rates of inflation, whereas in the second case we have a shortage of industrial investments, which are necessary for the maintenance of economic growth and employment; a choice between inflation and unemployment.

Monetary policy cannot solve economic problems on its own. It can only act as a brake to an inflationary path. It cannot act as an accelerator for economic expansion and development. This can only be achieved by the appropriate fiscal policy. For that reason, monetary policy is considered as a supplement to fiscal policy.

Monetary policy is much more complex and crucial than it seems. It may even become the principal cause of inflation! If real interest rates fall below 2% p.a. for a number of years, people may reduce their saving habits to an extent that cannot be reversed by subsequent changes in monetary policy while inflation is rising. Under such conditions it is necessary for real interest rates to rise above 3% p.a. and stay there for a long period of time (the experience of Greece in the early 1990's). Unfortunately, the maintenance of high real interest rates during the fight against inflation brings about a rate of increase in monetary growth above the rate of inflation (unless we have a budget surplus, which will lead to a tremendous increase in unemployment as in the early 1930's). At the same time, high real interest rates discourage consumption and industrial investments thereby restricting the future supply of goods while the supply of money is rising fuelling a future inflation. Thus, high real interest rates may lead not only to higher unemployment but also to higher inflation!

In summary, high rates of inflation call for high real interest rates. In such a case, however, high real interest rates also imply very high nominal interest rates. Unfortunately, exceptionally high nominal interest rates bring about a large increase in the supply of money. In the mean time, high real interest rates restrict any increase in the level of consumption and industrial investments. This in turn restricts the production and supply of goods to the domestic market while the supply of money continuously increases. Before long, the large increase in the supply of money brings about an increase in the demand for goods for which domestic production is not prepared. That implies higher market prices (i.e. inflation) and an increase in imports which may lead to a large trade deficit and subsequently to a fall in the value of the domestic currency in the foreign exchange markets (another cause of inflation). Thus, high inflation rates cause high interest rates and vice versa! Then, they may both become parts of a vicious circle (or vicious spiral) which can only be broken by a package of drastic measures supported by the appropriate fiscal policies. The principal cost of monetary stabilisation, however, should be born by those most responsible for the increases in market prices (i.e. the producers and wholesalers) and in interest rates (i.e. the bankers) and not by the general public.

The competitive edge of bankers over all other businesses should also be cut by levying a tax on all bank deposits (private and corporate) at the rate of at least 2% p.a. (or more, if necessary). The above tax should not affect the interest paid on bank deposits (as it could well be paid by the banks drawing on their balances with the central bank) and could be used to cover future bankrupties in the financial sector (i.e. an insurance rate on bank deposits paid by the banks).

The above turmoil would have been avoided had the government adopted the proposed taxation system, for it eliminates the conditions for high inflation and interest rates. But the new system presumes a political courage and determination to solve the principal socioeconomic problems at the least possible social cost without regard to the particular interests of those mostly responsible (i.e. the richest) or to the personal cost of political decisions (the price to be paid may be as high as life itself!)

Inflation is no longer a major problem for the advanced economies. Unfortunately, the same cannot be said for unemployment. Millions of workers lose their jobs every year without the possibility of finding new ones soon. World unemployment already exceeds 10% of the available labour force (in some countries is over 20%) and is expected to rise still further in the near future. In addition, more than 1 billion "free" people still live in conditions worse than those designed for the criminal convicts in the welfare states (during the Great Depression many unemployed workers in Chicago were breaking shop windows in order to secure food and accommodation in a state prison!) And all this is taking place when man is flying high in space and stepping on the moon; when man can see and talk with someone who lives thousands of miles away; when man can have breakfast in Tokyo and dinner in Paris on the same day. Nevertheless, about 50% of the world population still lives in conditions as bad as those found in the East End of London and in Bronx, New York. The rest of the world population seems to be enjoying the present. The majority of the property owners is not prepared to share even a small portion of what they have with those who have nothing. Besides, they would feel much better if they were relieved from the burdens of taxation, if they had more money, if they had more of everything!

They do not mind if they can only have junk food and plastic clothes, if they drive their fancy cars in dirty streets and send their children to schools surrounded by drug dealers. Unfortunately these dealers also share the same dream: to have more and more! "Gain" is the name of the game.

Possession seems to satisfy not only physiological needs but also psychological ones! In the minds of some people it seems to be associated with personal vigour and achievement. Insignificant men in every respect pose as important members of society by demonstrating possession of luxuries. They may spend a fortune in order to acquire something that will stir the wonder of friends and enemies, contestants in a struggle for precious possessions. But not a word for a salary increase to their servants.

It seems that some men are possessed by an insatiable desire to possess! Then, acquiring becomes their main goal in life. Possessed by strong gravitational forces known as greed, they demonstrate an attraction for everything that lies in their vicinity, from food and drinks to public attention! If they had the capacity they would consume everything. They are the black holes of society.

Every generation must have produced by the time it passes away at least as much as it has consumed, otherwise mankind will return back to the Stone Age. Similarly, every individual must have produced in value by the time of his death at least as much as he has consumed. Unfortunately, some people produce nothing or very little during their life time either because they die too young or because they are born very rich. On the other hand, many people who work hard throughout their life leave behind fortunes to be enjoyed by their descendants. But making fortunes is not man's destiny (this would reduce man to an ant). No species can survive long on bad terms with nature. Man cannot be an exception, for he is nothing more than a small part of nature, an embryo in her womb called Earth. Therefore, man has to live in harmony with nature and observe her laws. He must also be in harmony with himself (i.e. happy) and his fellow men. Apart from food, he needs love and affection (basic psychological* needs).

* Physiological and psychological needs are not interchangeable: "You cannot buy love" (Love must not be confused with flirt or sexual intercourse; "falling in love" actually raises men and women above the level of beasts).

In a society that claims to be civilized and does justice to its members, all adults should participate in the production process to the best of their ability, and then share in the fruits of labour in proportion to their social contribution. In any case, work should be both a right and a duty (a right to be employed and a duty to work). In this respect, the current levels of world unemployment are unacceptable to a civilized man; they must be brought down as soon as possible.

Since current economic growth rates are not sufficient to absorb all "surplus" labour, employment time should be reconsidered. The 40 hour week adopted by American industrialists more than 100 years ago, when industry was still in its early age, seems to be now out of proportion with the present capacity of the world economy. Besides, current market demand is more concerned with quality rather than quantity. This calls for the use of advanced technological equipment by a well trained highly educated labour force. As a result, productivity has become a matter of industrial expertise rather than work time length. On the other hand, it has long been proved by industrial psychologists that employment time length has only marginal effects on total production levels after a certain point. It has long been found that a full time worker tends to produce less in proportion to a part time worker, as fatigue tends to lower the efficiency of workers after 5 hours of continuous effort. The experience in excommunist countries also suggests that long working days do not necessarily produce more commodities. For many reasons, the length of the working day should be reduced to 6 hours for manual workers and 7 hours for office workers without any reduction in wages and salaries. In addition, overtime work should be reduced to certain professions such as seamen, firemen and doctors (on an annual basis they should not be employed for more hours than any other worker).

The reduction of the working day will be beneficial not only to the workers themselves but also to the society as a whole. The extra free time could be used for their intellectual development, for cultural activities, for sports, for looking after their mates and children, or for doing some housework. It is worth mentioning that the ancient Greek civilization owes much of its growth to the abundance of free time that was available to all citizens throughout the year (slaves excluded!) Those citizens, despite their privileged position in society, did not enjoy more food, better clothes or housing than today's middle class families in the developed countries. Nevertheless, civilization has not progressed much ever since, despite the tremendous technological development after the industrial revolution.

Obviously, there must be something wrong with our way of life. Today most people do not use their brains much outside work. They work too much and think too little. They are the slaves of the industrial society, of the market economy. A few decades ago Albert Einstein pointed out that the most underdeveloped part of the world was the human intellect! And it still remains so. And it will continue to remain so until people devote enough time to exercise their intellect on a daily basis as they do with their bodies in the gymnasiums. But in a society where some people are born with everything and the rest with very little or nothing, the free development of everybody's intellect prepares the ground for political demands towards a truly progressive taxation system without loop-holes for the wealthy and for the creation of a state that serves the entire population rather than the large property owners, or the financiers.

The reduction of the working day may reduce business profits in the short term but it will also reduce the budget deficit via the increase in income tax revenues and the decrease in unemployment benefits. The decrease in PSBR (Public Sector Borrowing Requirement) will help reduce the National Debt and the level of interest rates. This will in turn improve the financial position of indebted companies and encourage industrial investments and innovations. The latter will raise industrial productivity and increase long-term business profits. Thus, the reduction in the working day will eventually lead to an increase in industrial output and business profits! Moreover, the return of the economy to levels of full employment will reduce poverty and crime, improve social and industrial relations and raise the general standard of living. The present socioeconomic differences among the population will be considerably reduced while a significant step will have been taken towards a more prosperous society.

Labour productivity will also improve if the workers have a significant share in the profits of the enterprise. Payment of relatively high wages or salaries is not enough. It is necessary to have a real commitment to the objectives of the enterprise. In this respect, profit sharing can provide a strong incentive for working harder and more carefully. However, it must not discourage industrial investments or divert funds to enterprises that reject profit sharing schemes. For those reasons, the following profit sharing scheme seems most appropriate.

10% of the net profits before tax to be equally distributed to all full-time employees who worked for the enterprise throughout the year.

Another 10% of the net profits before tax to be distributed to the above employees in proportion to their annual payroll (Salaries over $100.000 p.a. to be excluded from the scheme).

Payment to be effected before the end of the first half of the following accounting year.

The profits so distributed to be taxed as ordinary income (i.e. as income from wages and salaries).

The profits so distributed to be listed (i.e. presented separately) on the respective financial statements of the enterprise.

The scheme is voluntary.

With respect to the public sector, there would be considerable benefits in terms of efficiency and quality service if most officials before assuming positions of authority had already gained some experience with large private companies, where they would have the chance to see with their own eyes how the private sector is organised and how people work and behave under competitive conditions. They should work there as assistant managers so that they could have a comprehensive view of the business. Then, they would have a better understanding of the issues facing the private sector. Thus, it would be beneficial for both sectors of the economy if high ranking officials at the Labour Department had already worked in the personnel departments of private companies, at the Board of Trade in supermarkets, at the Department of Industry as assistants to production managers in manufacturing firms, at the Treasury as assistants to chief accountants in banks etc. The above "industrial training" period should involve all civil servants with advanced education and be part of a comprehensive manpower development programme for civil servants aimed at improving labour performance throughout the country. The programme should be backed by legislation which provides for the following.

All medium and large sized companies and firms to participate (enterprises employing less than 100 people to be excluded).

2% of the total number of employees to be civil servants who work as assistant mangers in the various departments (the personnel and accounting departments to employ at least 2 trainees, 1 each.

The civil servants to work for the benefit of the company and at the instructions of their superiors (i.e. company managers and directors).

The "industrial training" period to be one year with each company. At the end of the year a report to be made by their company superiors concerning their overall performance and sent to the respective ministries. The reports should also contain the trainees' comments on the organisation and performance of the enterprises, their recommendations to improve business operations, productivity etc.

In case of illegal actions committed by company managers and directors (i.e tax evasion, unpaid overtime) the trainees would have to report those actions to their ministries without delay (a copy of the report to be sent to the minister himself).

Their salary to be jointly paid by their private employer and the state. (The company to pay only the minimum salary for office workers, the rest to be paid by the state).

After the end of the industrial training period, they would have no right to work for the same company again even after they have left the public sector.

Undoubtedly, the above programme provides a good framework for substantial improvements in productivity and efficiency in both sectors of the economy. Despite that, it should not be expected to gain the support of tax evaders, fraudulent entrepreneurs, and sly politicians, who want to keep the big business outside the scope of the public.

At the dawn of the 21st century, the largest part of the world is ruled by the richest 1.000 families. In spite of what we may think, our way of life principally depends on their choice, good or bad. They determine, to a large extent, the content of public speech, for they own most of the press. They set the standards of social conduct, for they own most of the T.V. stations. They determine the major political issues, for they are the major financial supporters of the leading politicians and movements. In the end, they not only direct public opinion to their own ends but also determine most of our private values and thoughts. Furthermore, they decide where we may work and therefore live; what we may produce and therefore consume. Finally, they fix our pay and therefore our standard of living. Thus, in practice the billionaire carries a right which is worth, 1.000.000 times as much as that of the ordinary citizen. Nevertheless, in the eyes of the law they are both equal!

Under the prevailing socioeconomic differences, the prospects of mankind are not particularly bright. Whether we like it or not, a choice has to be made between the billionaires on one side and the rest of the society on the other. Since history has proved that a society can survive and prosper without a royal family, we have every reason to believe that we can also live and prosper without industrial, financial and commercial barons. What they are, after all, is what we, the people, let them be!

TABLE OF MACROECONOMIC THEORY AND PRACTICE			
COMMUNISM	**SOCIALISM**	**CAPITALISM**	**INDIVIDUALISM**
Equality	Balance	Inequality	Divergence
Homogeneity	Variety	Contrast	Singularity
Comradeship	Contest	Competition	Conflict

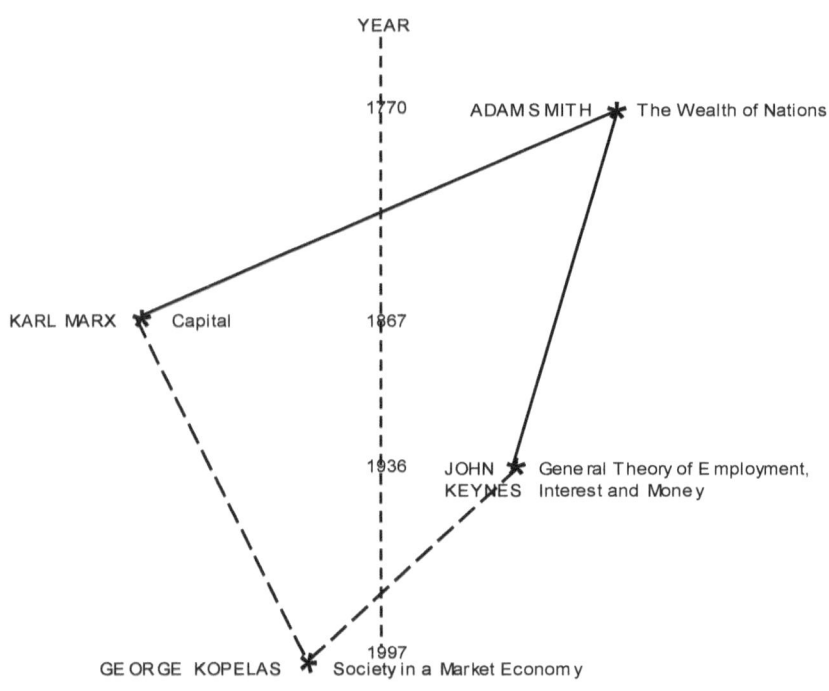

Useful Products of Current Intellectual Work

*Reality is not a matter of description**
Nothing stems from nowhere
Distance is a measure of space
Motion is the change of material positions in space
Time is a measure of motion
Velocity is a relationship between two distinct
Real motion is neither smooth nor steady
Motion is life, rest is death
Energy is the motion of matter
God is the energy of the universe
Man is a tiny part of the universe
Man is not allowed to break the laws of nature
Size, quantity, speed and quality are relative measures
Quality is a matter of quantitative relationships
The difference between energy and matter is a matter of speed
Thoughts are forms of brain energy
The human brain has the power of an atomic bomb
Thoughts without deeds are lamps without light
Reason is the road that seems to lead to the truth
The truth is an idea that corresponds to reality
The truth is not a matter of probabilities
The truth is like a diamond: precious and bright but hard to find
The truth is a choosy woman dressed in a dozen lies
The lie is a child of imagination
The imagination is a reflection of reality
* most of them are made by the author himself

The imagination is a child of personal experience

Light and imagination have the tendency to fill up the empty space

Equality and ideals are children of imagination

The discovery of the truth calls for a departure from the fascinating world of fiction

To know means to own the truth

Knowledge is a child of experience and reason

Knowledge is not only a matter of reason but also of spare time

Originality is not only a matter of free thinking but also of free time

Knowledge and money have a tendency to accumulate

Knowledge is a valuable friend

The value of knowledge is a matter of practice

Scientific knowledge is a set of truths

The truth and the lie are flatmates

Exaggerating is the most efficient way of lying

Advertising is the most profitable production of lies

Advertising makes everyone feel poorer

Television is the most beautiful drug

Television reduced not only the distance between people but also their size

Value is a matter of social contribution

Where the average is considered good, and the good excellent, the best disappear

We are what we do rather than what we think or say

Whatever we do affects both our surroundings and ourselves

The protection of the environment is the best legacy to our descendants

We are responsible not only for our actions but also for our omissions

No need, no life

The tombs are not made for the dead but for the living

The temples are made for the faithful and not for God

The religions are made by men and not by God

The religions are nothing more than dogmatic philosophies

Dogmatism is the mother of a dozen evils

The end does not justify the means

When the means become an end in itself, the end is lost

Even today most people still behave like our distant ancestors, they ape

Living with the past reduces the present, and living for the present reduces the future

If you want to enjoy the present you have to prepare for the future, for the present is a future of the past

The study of history is to serve the future, not the past

It is much harder to make history than read

The book is the glass of society

The book is the microscope of the intellectual

There are no average books

The value of a good book is much higher than its price

The true value of people and things is revealed during their absence

Appreciation is a matter of deprivation

You had better ask more from yourself and less from the others

We all owe something to the society

We all have a right to employment and a duty to work

To work means to serve society

Work is the mother of prosperity

The lust for possessions leads to prostitution

A keen possessor is a slave of passion

Worship means submission

The worship of money and wealth leads to crime and death

The uneven distribution of money and wealth leads a few people to Paradise and a lot to Hell

Lover of money, servant of wealth

Falling in love but rising to Heaven

Love begets freedom, worship begets slavery

Hypocricy is a sign of slavery

We are not masters of ourselves but slaves of our passion

Desire is the inertia of the living

No need, no life

The needy and the happy live in separate flats

Happiness is a matter of balance

To be happy is to be on good terms with yourself and the environment

If you want to find happiness you have to follow the tempo of nature

No respect for nature, no respect for people

We had better care more about the reaction of nature

Generosity is the mother of charity

Getting rich is not a charitable engagement

Man is driven either by love or by self-interest

To love someone is to share your happiness with one's misery

Love is the mother of happiness

Love has no choice

Love is a gift of the soul

Love is not for sale or rent

To sell means to offer for one's own benefit

Trade primarily serves the needs of the rich

Every dollar spent on the purchase of a good is also a vote for its production

Words can fill up the brain but not the stomach

If you eat too much you also eat your life

Too much of a good is bad

Over consumption is a sign of spiritual emptiness

Drug addiction is a side effect of over consumption

Taking drugs is the hard way to commit suicide

A society without welfare is a family without affection

Nothing against society may be just or right

Law and justice do not always sleep together

The law is a guide to social conduct rather than a guarantee for good behaviour

Social justice is a matter of means and opportunities

It is unfair to be born either rich or poor

Succession is the mother of class society

Succession is a time-bomb to the very foundations of democracy

It is much easier to make the rich richer than the poor rich

Money divides the poor and unites the rich

Money is a right

Money is a master key

The power of money lies in our deficiencies

Money cannot buy love or happiness

We all need more time and choice rather than money and voice

Freedom and choice are two sides of the same coin

Freedom is a matter of relative strength

Free are the mighty

The mighty are either worshipped or hated

Ownership determines freedom

Ownership is not a natural right but a social concession

Ownership is a child of greed and selfishness

The communist is the enemy of the selfish

A communist loves neither his things nor those who love them

If you love something more than people you can be a danger to humanity

The servants revolt, the masters reform

Capitalism is a shark that also lives on land

Money is the blood of capitalism

Political authority without economic power is a hand without fingers

Neo liberalism is the cocaine of the market economy

High short term profits often lead to long term losses

The excessive profits are cancerous

Profits beget wealth, and wealth begets profits

Unemployment is the canker of our society

In our competitive world most athletes still run barefoot

Competition is the salt of life

War is a deadly form of competition

State wars are large-scale robberies

Ruin is the only certain outcome of a war

The road to ruin is often decorated with impressive flags

It takes one to start a war but two to make peace

Civil war is a national wreck with sole survivors those most responsible, lucky and light

National campains abroad are exports of domestic economic problems

Nationalism and intolerance are the raw materials of the war industries

Fascism is the political demonstration of schizophrenia

Fascism is a child of autocracy and disorder

We are children not only of our parents but also of our own experiences

In our political opponents we often see our bad self rather than theirs

The political leader is an elected general of the citizens

There are two kinds of politicians: those who believe in certain ideals and those who trade in them

A politician without ideals is a skipper without a compass

The politicians represent the personal needs of their supporters but above all their own

The role of the leader is to show the way we had better follow and not to walk on our behalf

The capable leader usually drives a bulldozer rather than a bus

In a general election one may choose between some vision andthe status quo

If you decide not to vote, you only let someone else make a choice for you

A blank vote is a conservative vote

Authority is a difficult and demanding woman

An authority may be threatened by its victims but it is usually undermined by its servants

The greatest actors are not to be found in the theatre but in the centres of power

Political authority is not only a matter of economic power but also of intellectual dominance

www.ingramcontent.com/pod-product-compliance
Lightning Source LLC
Chambersburg PA
CBHW020346290526
45785CB00005B/2172